All Time Heroes

From All Times

~ Volume 8 ~

SAINT **SHENOUDA**PRESS

All Time Heroes
From All Times

~ Volume 8 ~

The Martyrdom of
Saint Mercurius
The General

ST SHENOUDA PRESS
SYDNEY, AUSTRALIA

2019

All Time Heros from all Times - Volume 8

The Martyrdom of Saint Mercurius the General

ST SHENOUDA PRESS

8419, Putty Rd,
Putty, NSW, 2330
Australia

www.stshenoudapress.com

ISBN 13: 978-0-6485754-3-6

Cover Design:
Hani Ghaly,
Begoury Graphics
begourygraphics@gmail.com

CONTENTS

The Martyrdom Of Saint Mercurius The General

Here begins the martyrdom of saint Mercurius, the general and martyr, the man glorious in Christ, the wearer of the crown in very truth, who completed his glorious strife on the twenty-fifth day of the month Hator. In the peace of God. May his holy blessing come upon us, and may we all be saved together. Amen.

INTRODUCTION

Truly, 'The light has risen upon the righteous,' in respect of this Saint Mercurius, according to the words which the sacred singer, the father of the Christ according to the flesh, the righteous king, the hymn-writer, David spoke. He cries out, he cries out with his sweet voice, and he sings to his harp saying, "The light has risen upon the righteous." And again he says, "The light has risen in the darkness for those who are right in their hearts." The Christ Himself says in the Gospel, "Then shall the righteous shine like the sun in the kingdom of their Father."

THE EMPEROR'S DECREE

At the time when Decius and Valerianus were reigning in the great city of Rome, they made a public decree and issued a general order to compel everyone, in every place, to offer up sacrifices and to pour out libations (offering of wine or oil) to the gods. Then Decius, the lawless Emperor, ordered the herald to make a proclamation throughout the whole city, saying, "Take heed, O all you people, whether soldier or peasant, and every man of every class and of every age whatsoever, and come, all of you, to the temple of the gods and offer up sacrifice to them there. Build strong altars at the gate of the temple, offer up sacrifices upon them, frankincense, and bulls, and goats, and feathered fowl, and let the firmament be filled full with the smoke of the heavy fumes of their burning carcases." And there was great trembling among the Christians, for the servants of Decius pursued them, and beat them, and dragged them to the gates of the temples, and to the secret shrines, and they compelled them to offer up sacrifices. There was very great trouble in every place, for the tyrant commanded his soldiers to produce before him every kind of terrifying instrument of torture in order that when the Christians saw them, they might fear the glittering swords, the iron beds, the instruments for drawing out the sinews, the knives for slitting and cutting out the tongue, the metal helmets, the sharp butcher's knives, the brazen cauldrons filled with boiling bitumen, the brazen cauldrons filled with boiling oil, the wheels with knives attached to it, all the other terrifying instruments of torture. The impious Emperor said, "Whoever shall resist my command I will gouge out his eyes, I will tear out his tongue, I will take out his entrails, I will cut through the soles of his feet, I will take out his brains, and the rest of his body I will give to the fire that it may consume it." When the men who were pious saw these things, great despair laid hold of them, and they were afraid and sighed in helplessness. Every man was delivering his neighbour over to death, fathers were delivering their sons over to death, brethren dragged out brethren delivering them over to death, for fear of the sword. Everyone who confessed the Name of Jesus was greatly distraught. When this imperial decree was published, the whole of the city of Rome was filled with quaking and fear, not only was the city of Rome troubled but likewise all the other cities, because this general order involved them also.

MERCURIUS GRANTED THE SWORD OF VICTORY

It came to pass at that time that war broke out among the Barbarians, who attacked the Romans. The Romans equipped their ships and made them ready to receive their troops to fight against the Barbarians. The Emperors ordered regiments from every district and city to come and assist them in battle. When they had arrived from all the various remote cities they prepared for war with all diligence. There was in the army a certain valiant young man whose name was Mercurius, and he was an officer in the Mareusian regiment, and he feared God. He was exceedingly goodly in appearance, and the whole army loved him because of his intelligence and manners. He was by race a native of Cappadocia, and he was a Christian from his childhood, born to Christian parents. He was a mighty man in battle, and God was with him in all his works. When the Tribune saw that he was far advanced in his knowledge of the theory and practice of the craft of the soldier, he made him a commander of his regiment. When the Emperor saw the valour of the young man he loved him, cleaved to him, and took counsel from him about the affairs of the Government. It came to pass after these things when the persecution had spread abroad, that the heathen Barbarians revolted against the Romans. Emperor Decius and the whole Senate found themselves in a position of great difficulty, due to their great lack of troops and equipment. For the Barbarians had fought against them with such success that they captured the great country of Armenia which was on the frontier between them and the Romans. Emperor Decius commanded the soldiers of every troop and regiment to be called up to go to the war and to fight against the Barbarians. Then the Emperor reserved for his own command certain armies and regiments, and he marched out to do battle with the Barbarians. He crossed the Euphrates, the great river, which is on the frontiers of Armenia, and he conquered the Barbarians in the twinkling of an eye and defeated their king and his army. Decius thought that he had won the war through the Providence of his gods, and he rejoiced exceedingly, dismissing the soldiers to their quarters and giving them each large monetary rewards for their efforts. Decius celebrated a festival in every city which he passed on his return to Rome.

THE CALL FOR MARTYRDOM

It was at that time that the great valor of this nobleman, Saint Mercurius, the true believer, the commander of the Mareusian regiment, was revealed. He was a man who was perfect in his service of God, and in his daily life and speech, he practiced piety of every kind. The Word of God was sweeter than honey in his mouth. It came to pass that one night when he was sleeping among his troops, that an angel of the Lord stood over him, touched his side, and awoke him. The angel had a sword in his right hand, his appearance was awe-inspiring and he was arrayed in the attire of war which was marvellous to behold. When Saint Mercurius saw him he was greatly afraid. The angel answered saying, "Mercurius". Mercurius opened his eyes and seeing the angel he was greatly afraid, thinking he was speaking to one of the imperial officers or a general. The angel handed him the sword which was in his hand saying to him, "Take this drawn sword, for by means of it you will destroy the whole army of the Barbarians. I am the Commander-in-Chief of the hosts of the Lord. I have come to help you and your fellow soldiers who believe in the Lord Jesus the Christ. Now, therefore, conquer and prevail, for I will be with you until the end of your strife, in peace. Behold, the time has come, and behold, the contest is arranged. Strive in such a way that you may receive your strength, for no athlete receives the crown unless he has striven persistently, or the farmer who has toiled strenuously is he who receives the fruits first.

Now, therefore, hear the words which I shall speak to you, do not delay to place your confidence in the Lord your God. For a mighty war is prepared for you and you shall be a valiant martyr. The fame of your martyrdom shall be spread abroad throughout the whole world, and everyone who hears about it shall marvel at your valour, glorifying God because of the mighty deeds, miracles, and works which our Lord God will perform through you. Great tortures await you at the hands of the lawless Emperor and cruel tribulations; but endure patiently, for you shall receive an incorruptible crown. Whoever builds a shrine in your name, and gives an offering in your name on the day of your commemoration, on them will I bestow my blessing and happiness in their habitations.

Behold I will bestow upon you three crowns; one for your riches, one for the sufferings which you have endured in My Name, and one for your virginity. Be strong and prevail, for I am with you." And when the angel had said these things to him, he went up into heaven surrounded with splendour.

The next morning Emperor Decius commanded his officers to prepare the troops in battle armor and prepare to attack the Barbarians in battle. Then the truly valiant man Saint Mercurius set out to attack the host of the Barbarians, and he rushed in among them through the power of God which was with him. He lifted up his eyes to heaven and saw the Archangel Michael, who was in the form of a general of the army. There was a drawn sword in his right hand, and he reached it out to Saint Mercurius, saying to him, "Be of good cheer! Take this sword, and make your way to the Barbarians, and slaughter them with it in the Name of the Christ Who shall give strength to you." And Saint Mercurius stretched out his hand and took the sword from the hand of the Archangel Michael, and he set out for the hosts of the Barbarians. He slaughtered them in the Name of the Christ, giving them no quarter until his hand stuck to the sword by reason of the great quantity of blood upon it. He destroyed the Barbarians with an exceedingly great and severe slaughter that day. The remnant fled and made themselves scarce. When the Emperor saw the deeds of valour which Saint Mercurius performed, through the strength of God, which was with him, he rejoiced exceedingly over the victory and the conquest which the Romans had gained. And the Emperor bestowed on Saint Mercurius great honours and very many possessions, and he determined to make him the captain of the Mareusian regiment.

MERCURIUS CONFESSES HIS FAITH IN CHRIST

It came to pass after these things that Emperor Decius commanded all his army, all the troops and their companies, the generals, the patricians, all the Romans of senatorial rank, to assemble in the temple of Apollo to offer up a sacrifice. Then, when the blessed man perceived the grievous error which had obtained dominion over the emperor and over the army through the Devil, he withdrew himself from them and made supplication to the Lord, saying, "O Lord Almighty, the Father of our Lord Jesus Christ, take good heed to Your clay which You have fashioned, and scatter abroad the stumbling-blocks which the Devil has cast into the hearts of all mankind. Establish the hearts of the people who fear Your Holy Name. O Lord, give strength to Your Church, so that everyone may believe in Your Holy Name. Glory be to You, and to Your Good Father, and to the Holy Spirit, forever and ever. Amen."

And it came to pass that when the emperor had come to the door of the temple, the whole army was gathered together inside it to offer up sacrifice, each one according to his rank. When it came to the turn of Saint Mercurius to offer up sacrifice, he was not to be found among the soldiers. When the Emperor had sought for him, he found him in his house sitting in sackcloth and ashes, grieving exceedingly over the great schism which had arisen throughout the entire world through the Devil. Then certain of the soldiers of the regiment of Mercurius made their way to the Emperor, creating accusations against the blessed Mercurius, saying, "O our Lord Emperor, live forever! Your glorious sovereignty has commanded all classes of men to offer up sacrifices to the glorious gods. Behold now, there are those who are near to you who are attached to your personal service, who treat your glorious decree with contempt, that is to say, Mercurius, who is under the rule of your kingdom, and whom you exalted to honour and have bestowed upon him the rank of Captain, setting him over the regiment. So great is this honor that the whole of the Roman army, when it heard of it, glorified him, making itself subject to him. Behold, he has treated your sovereign power with contempt by not joining us in the temple to offer up sacrifices to the gods, but he has gone into his house. We found him in his house, sitting in sackcloth and ashes, and praying to the Lord his God with tears. He was persuading everyone to turn away from the worship of the gods and to follow Jesus the Nazarene, whom they crucified, saying, "It is He Who is God; He created the heavens and the earth".

And the Emperor spoke to those who related these things to him saying, "These things which you say to me about Mercurius, who was attached to me, to the effect that he treated me with contempt, may be true; nevertheless, let two of the officers who are here go and summon him, so that I may know that these things which you say to me about him are in truth or not." Then they brought the blessed Mercurius into the presence of Emperor Decius. His eyes were filled with tears, he was arrayed in the garb of humiliation, and they set him in the presence of the Emperor. When Decius saw him in the garb of humiliation he shook his head, finding it difficult to understand what had happened to him. He spoke to Mercurius, saying, "Mercurius, tell me what has happened to you, what excuse do you have for treating with contempt the great honours which I have bestowed upon you. I held you to be worthy of the forethought of the gods, and you have counted as trash the high rank which I placed you in. The whole of the Roman army is assembled in the temple to offer sacrifice to the righteous gods, and it is you only who have separated yourself from the troops. Further, tell me what the country of which you are a native is. Did your parents call you by this name Mercurius?"

PHILOPATIR 'LOVER OF THE FATHER'

And the blessed Mercurius answered and said to the Emperor, "You wish to know of what country I am a native: listen, then, I will tell you about my origin. I am a native of Cappadocia, so far as this world is concerned; but as for my own native city, I belong to the heavenly Jerusalem, the mother city of the saints. The name which my parents gave to me originally was Philopatir, which means "Lover of the Father", but when I became a soldier I was called Mercurius by the commander of my regiment. I am a servant of Jesus the Christ, my Lord, the Son of the Living God." When the Emperor heard these things he remained stunned for a very considerable time. He shook his head, saying, "Cast away from you this silly boasting and this mad idea of yours, get into the temple and offer up a sacrifice to the great god Apollo.

Then get back to your troop, where your fellow soldiers are and take up your rank and duty as before." The holy man Mercurius said to the lawless Emperor, "Let this fact be quite plain before you, O lawless Emperor: I will not offer up sacrifice to your god Apollo, that vain thing, and forsake my God, Who is the Creator of the heavens and the earth, and of everything in it. For I am a Christian. To the liberty and the life of the soldier of this world I bid farewell, and as for the high rank which you gave me I do not need it. I am a servant of the Christ Jesus, the Son of the Living God."

Emperor Decius answered and said to him, "Mercurius, up to the present I did not believe the things which your accusers told me concerning you, for I knew well how envious they were of you who made accusations against you, and that they did so because they saw the great honour which I had conferred upon you over the whole regiment. Now, therefore, listen to me: Sacrifice to the gods. Do not force me to forget our friendship and to strip you of your rank, and inflict severe tortures upon you." The blessed Mercurius answered and said to the Emperor, "The friendship of this world is of no account whatsoever, it is a thing unfavourable to God. Similarly, these honours are for a season only, but the glory of God endures forever. Now, therefore, do not trouble yourself, for I am a Christian, I will not offer up a sacrifice to your abominable god, whatever you wish to do to me, do." Decius said to him, "O Mercurius, offer up sacrifice and do not die a terrible death." The blessed Mercurius said to him, "O Emperor, let this one word be sufficient for you. I will not obey you and serve strange gods, and cast my God, Jesus the Christ, behind my back."

MERCURIUS TORTURED

When Decius heard these things he was exceedingly angry. He commanded them to strip off his apparel and made the soldiers lay him on the ground and beat him with leather whips. ; They did so until the ground was soaked with his blood. Decius the Emperor said to him, "Mercurius, you find tortures to be troublesome things. Are they worse than you offering of sacrifice or not?" The blessed Mercurius answered, saying, "As long as I have with me my Lord Jesus Christ to help me, I shall not sink under your tortures. For I am a servant of my Lord Jesus Christ, Who helps me, Who is the King of what is in heaven and of what is on the earth."

When Emperor Decius heard these things he said, "Mercurius, listen to me. Offer sacrifice to the gods, and avoid these terrible tortures, in order that you may not die an evil death. Up to this point I have had compassion upon you, I have been long-suffering with you. For I did not wish to do you harm, especially because you were my friend during the attack which happened to us in the war. Listen to me, offer up a sacrifice to the gods. Do not destroy your youth with these severe tortures. I am considering our friendship in speaking these things." The blessed Mercurius answered and said, "Every suffering which shall be to me through confessing my God will add to my holy reward, for the sufferings of this present time are not worthy of the glory which shall be revealed to us." When the Emperor Decius heard these things he said to Mercurius, "Since you have established in your heart these foolish words and consider Roman honours to be of no value, and will not obey the Imperial Law, I will punish you according to your foolishness; I shall see whether the God in Whom you believe can save you from my hands." Saint Mercurius said to the Emperor, it is written in the Book of the Holy Apostle, "Who shall separate us from the love of God? Not tribulation, or affliction, or persecution, or hunger, or nakedness, or danger, or the sword. Even as it is written, "For Your sake, they slay us all day long. For we are persuaded that neither death, nor life, nor angel, nor principality, nor power, nor things which are nor things which shall be, shall be able to separate us from the love of the Christ."

When the blessed Mercurius had said these things Emperor Decius was furious, and he commanded his men to put Mercurius on the rack (stretching machine) and torture him. The executioners stretched him until the bones of his back were pulled to pieces, yet the blessed man never ceased to bless God, saying, "O Lord Jesus the Christ, the Only-begotten of the Father, Who were born of the holy virgin Mary, Who took flesh upon Yourself of the true lamb, and in the end delivered the whole race of Adam, setting us free from the slavery of our sins. I give thanks to You that You have made us worthy of Your great goodness. Hear me this day. I am Your servant Mercurius. Make me worthy of Your invitation, of the partaking in Your holy sufferings, and of the faithful witness of Your Godhead. Now, therefore, O my Lord, do not forsake me and do not go far from me, for tribulations await me, and fetters have fallen upon me. Give me strength, O my Lord, until I have finished my contest in peace. Do not let my enemies rejoice over me, and do not let them say among the unbelievers, "Where is their God?" When he had said these things, behold, a voice came to him, saying, "Be of good cheer, O my athlete Mercurius. Bear patiently, O My chosen hero, for I will be with you, I will give strengthen you and

protect you. I will help you in every suffering which you will
endure in My Name. Do not be dismayed, I will be with you;
I will give you strength until you have completed your contest
bravely." Then the angel made the Sign of the Cross over his
whole body, and immediately the rack split and became two
parts, and the fetters with which he was bound were burst in
pieces. Mercurius stood on his feet, with no injury on him on
the contrary and he was continuously glorifying God.

And when the Emperor saw what had taken place, he was
filled with wrath, and he said, "Since this man said, 'We have
armour in which to fight,' I hereby give the order for him to
be stretched out on four stakes, and to suspend him between
heaven and earth one cubit (about 50cm)." When they had
done this to him the Emperor said, "Where is the armour in
which you fight, in which you put your trust? I swear by the
greatest of the gods, Zeus, that you have been well handled."
The holy man looked up into heaven and said, "O Lord, help
me, I am Your servant." The Emperor further commanded
them to make gashes in his body with sharp knives and goads
of iron, and afterward to sprinkle burning coals of fire upon
him, so that little by little he might be consumed. When they
did these things the fiery coals were extinguished by the blood
which flowed from the righteous man. The holy man bore

this new torture with great courage. Decius made them carry him away, saying, "Let him die quickly"; and the soldiers took him away into a place of darkness. When they were carrying him away he was lifeless, but there was a little breath left in him, although they all thought he was dead.

Behold, a very short time later, the angel of the Lord appeared to him, and said, "Peace be to you, O you mighty athlete!" When he had said this, he healed the wounds which were in his body, gave him the strength to stand so that he stood up and glorified God. After these things, the Emperor made them bring him before the tribunal. When the Emperor saw him, he said, "Have you been rescued from my hands? You were half dead! How can you now walk?" He commanded his spearmen to examine his body carefully, and they said to the Emperor, "We swear by your own power, O pious Emperor, that his entire body is in a healthy state, that there is no sign of harm upon it, and that it is as if it had never been touched." Decius said, "Surely he will say, "It was Christ Who healed me." Did you not take a physician into the prison to treat him with medicines?" They said, "By your glorious majesty which rules the whole world, it was none of the men who heal that cured him. We thought that he would surely die, how he is alive and how he has been revived we do not know. The magic of the Christians is exceedingly powerful. Yesterday he was a dead man, and today he stands up whole and well." The Emperor was filled with wrath, and he said to Mercurius, "Tell me truly who it was that healed you without magic." Saint Mercurius answered and said, "It was my Lord Jesus, the Christ, the Physician of souls and bodies, who bestowed a cure upon me: for it is said, "The man who uses magical schemes, the men who use incantations, the worshippers of idols shall be strangers to Him; and He shall bind them with fetters that cannot be broken, and shall deliver them over to the everlasting fire, because they did not know their Creator."

And the Emperor said, "I am going to inflict the most terrible tortures upon your body; let me see if the Christ, on Whom you believe, will heal you." Saint Mercurius said, "I believe on my Lord Jesus, the Christ; even though you will inflict multitudes of punishments upon me, you will not move me. For He said, "Fear not those who can kill your bodies, but who have no power to kill your souls but fear Him Who has the power to destroy both your souls and your bodies." Then the Emperor commanded the executioners to bring a red-hot iron and apply it to his members and to apply blazing torches to his rib. When they had done this, instead of smoke, a sweet aroma arose and it spread about among all those who were in that place. Now although they tortured him horribly, he neither uttered a groan nor wept. The Emperor said to him, "Where is your Physician now? Let Him come and heal you. You also said If I die He is able to raise me up again." Saint Mercurius said to him, "Do whatever you wish. For you have power over my body, but God is the master of my soul. Even if you destroy my body, my soul shall endure." The Emperor further ordered them to hang his head downwards and to bring a large stone and suspend it from his neck, so that he might suffocate and die quickly. The power of God dwelt in the martyr, and he endured for a long time under this punishment.

Mercurius Martyred

When Emperor Decius saw that he bore the pain with great strength and that the torture in no way affected him, he ordered them to remove the stone which was attached to his neck and bring a leather whip with four thongs and to beat him until the ground under him was saturated with his blood. The nobleman endured this torture also, like a solid stone in his courage. Mercurius said, "I give thanks to You, O my Lord, that You have held me to be worthy to suffer for Your holy Name." When the Emperor saw that his determination was immovable and that he could not persuade him to offer up a sacrifice to the gods, he came to a decision, for it was urgent for him to go to Rome, and he passed the sentence of death on him. He ordered them to kill him with the sword saying, "Mercurius, having treated the gods with scorn and despised the holy dogma of our gods, esteemed our power of no account, I hereby command that he be taken to the city of Cappadocia and that he be beheaded there, in the sight of all men. For everyone who, having received honour from the Emperor decides to then contradict his command, shall receive stripes and be delivered over to the sword." They journeyed on the high road, and after a few days, they reached the city of Caesarea. The Lord stood by him and said to him, "Mercurius, come, take your rest with Me, since you have finished your course, and have kept the faith; receive the crown of an athlete, that which has been allotted to you, you will inherit." When the Lord had appeared to him, the martyr became strong, and he said to those who were in charge of him, "Do quickly that which you have been commanded to do. The Lord Who calls every man to repentance shall make you be worthy of His grace. He is rich and gracious to those who go to Him willingly, without a wicked will". When he had said these things, they took off his head and he completed the good confession of our Saviour on the twentieth day of

November, which is Hator.

A great miracle took place which is worthy of mention. After the martyr had ended his course his body became as white as snow, and it emitted a sweet smell which was like choice incense. Because of this sign, very many men became Christians. The holy man was laid in a prominent place, in which very many works of power and miracles were performed on his account.

Glory be to God the Father, and to His Only-begotten Son, Jesus the Christ, our Lord, and to the Holy Spirit, now and always, forever and ever. Amen.

THE MIRACLES OF SAINT MERCURIUS THE GENERAL

THE FIRST MIRACLE

This is the miracle which was manifested through Saint Mercurius; how the saint smote Julian, the lawless Emperor with his spear (the account of it is written in the ninth section of the History of the Church). At the time when Cyril was bishop of Jerusalem, a mighty sign of Christ was made manifest. From the third until the ninth hour of the day (9 am to 3 pm), a great cross of light appeared standing above the grave of the Saviour, in the sight of all flesh, both believers and unbelievers, Barbarian and Romans. It was so wonderful that all the multitudes who lived in the city gathered together with their meat, and their drink, and their wine, and while they were eating they gazed upon the cross until it ascended into heaven at about the ninth hour.

Cyril, the Bishop of Jerusalem, wrote an account of the miracle which had taken place and wrote a letter to emperor Kostos (Constantius), emperor of the Province in which Athanasius resided. Athanasius ruled over the Church of Rakote (Alexandria) for twenty years, with no strife or controversy arising against him throughout his reign. When the Emperor Kostos died, Julian became his successor. Julian was a lawless pagan, a descendant from the sister of

Constantine the Great, whose husband was also a pagan. The sons of Constantine saw that the young man Julian had a courageous spirit and a beautiful voice. Fearing voice and fearing that he could not endure the demands of the empire, they gave him to the Church to fulfil the role of a reader. Certain men of his father's household led him into paganism. When Constantius had died, Julian reigned as his successor. Julian gave himself over to paganism, seeking to open the temples with the general consent of the public. Now Julian dwelt in the palace of Antioch, for he was unworthy to dwell in the buildings which had been occupied by Constantine. He went into a worshipping place of the pagans, took a hawk and gave it to the priest for offering as a sacrifice to the idol. The priest took out the liver of the hawk and gave it to Julian, who ate it.

At that time the Church was rich in the valour of the men, who were arrayed in the Spirit. The church was supported by four pillars, namely: Athanasius of Rakote, Anthony and Pachomius in the southern country, and Basilius in Cappadocia. Basilius was a friend of Julian because they had spent their childhood together in school. When Basilius heard of Julian's evil deeds he went to visit him together with other God-worshipping friends from his diocese. When they had entered into Julian's presence, Julian saw the humility of their condition, with meek appearances and long beards, he remarked, "What are these men seeking after?" Basilius answered and said, "We are seeking after a shepherd who will be good to his flocks". The Emperor said to Basilius "Where have you left the Son of the carpenter, that you come here?" Basilius replied, "I have left Him making a chest for you wherein you shalt be cast into hell." The Emperor said to him, "I will avoid entering into a debate on our differences because I value our friendship and do not want to be forced to have your head cut off." Basilius said to him, "You are not a philosopher. If you were a philosopher, you would not cast behind your back the wisdom which you learnt when you were a reader of the books of the true wisdom." The Emperor said to him, "I read them, and I understood them." Basilius said to the Emperor, "You neither read them carefully nor did you understand them if you had understood them you would never have reviled them." The Emperor said to them, "I will shut you up until I have arrived in Persia, and I will make you know what it is to oppose the Emperor. You shall be filled with affliction in prison." Basilius said, "If you go into Persia and return, then has God not spoken by Basilius." Julian said, "What shall I do to the Galilean, the liar? He said in His heart, they shall not leave one stone upon another in

the Temple of the Jews. I myself will build an imperial palace,
I will make His word to be a lie, and I will show you that He
is a liar."

The Emperor commanded Basilius and the other two
men who were with him to be thrown in prison while he
embarked on his expedition into Persia. He came to Jerusalem,
and he saw the ruins of the Temple, that there was not one
wall standing round about it. It was in the same state as when
Vespasian destroyed it at the time of the destruction which he
wrought against the Jews. Julian commanded his servants to
clear out the place in order that he might build an exceedingly
splendid palace there. He appointed a count over the Temple
who should clear the site so that he might lay the foundations
and build the palace. He went to Persia and waged war there.
Meanwhile, he left the holy men locked in prison. They cleared
out the ruins of the Temple, of which not one stone remained
that had not been torn away from the other, according to the
word of our Saviour. They began to build, working on the
building from sunrise to sunset. When the workmen arrived
in the morning they found that which had been built up the
day before collapsed, however, it was evident that it was not
done at the hand of man. They continued to work for two
months with the same result. They were miserable, for their

work did not progress, according to the Divine Providence that hindered them. The Jews there spoke to the workmen, saying, "Burn the tombs in which the Christians have buried bodies, then you will be able to build". They listened to them and burned the tombs. When they came to the tombs where John the Baptist and Elisha the Prophet were buried, the fire would not touch them. For a large period of time fire filled the region around them, but it would not touch them. Certain brethren gave to him money and entreated him to allow them to take away the bones of the holy men. He let them have their will and made them come by night and carry away the bones of the holy men John the Baptist and Elisha the Prophet. The hand of the Lord was with them, and they were moved to take the bones to Egypt to Athanasius because he desired to see them. They came to the sea, and they embarked in a ship hurriedly. They sailed and came to Rakote very quickly, and they gave the bones to Athanasius. He rejoiced over them as if he could see them, that is to say as if he were looking upon John the Baptist and Elisha in the flesh. He hid the bones in the baptistery and looked forward to the time when he would be able to build a memorial for them.

Saint Athanasius used to eat by day in the garden of our fathers with the brethren, and daily he invited the chief clergy to go there. They did not only eat, but they listened also to the words of wisdom which God had given to him, according to that which is written, "Everything to the glory of God." Whether at the moment of fasting, or at the moment of eating or drinking, he ate, and he drank by the word of God at all times. He ate then with the brethren, with the clergy, and with the chief 'lovers of work' of the Church in the garden which he had in the quarter of the city which was called 'Hermes', situated to the south of the city. It was open towards the dunghills and the open spaces formed by waste ground. He was accustomed to saying, "If I can find the time I will clear away the dunghills and will build on the site where they stand a memorial to John the Baptist." At that moment Theophilus was standing by the table eating because he acted as secretary to him, he heard the words which Athanasius said, pondering them in his heart. Julian, as he was impelled by wrath to go to Persia, went there, where God delivered him into the hands of the Persians because he had left the holy men locked in prison when he departed to Persia.

The death that he died took place as follows: He saw one night a multitude of soldiers coming against him in the air, and, behold, a spear transfixed him in his loins, and he knew that they (i.e. the soldiers) were the holy men (Mercurius and his friends). He took his blood and threw it up towards heaven, saying, "Take this, O Christ, for You have taken the whole world." Having uttered this blasphemy he immediately fell down, and God took away his rule from the people, delivered us, and the Romans occupied their country. Three days before the death of Julian, Basilius in prison saw a vision. He awoke and spoke to his companions, saying, "This night I have seen the holy martyr, Saint Mercurius. He went into his martyrium, and drawing forth his spear said, "Shall I permit this lawless man to blaspheme the God of heaven in this manner?" Having said these words he departed, and I ceased to see him." The two companions of Basilius answered, saying, "In very truth we also ourselves have just seen this very same vision." When they perceived this purpose which God had shown them they believed, saying to each other, "Let us send into the memorial of Saint Mercurius and see if his spear is fixed in its place or not." They sent and finding not the spear they believed in the vision. After three days letters were sent to Antioch, saying, "The king has died in battle." As the result of a vote directed by God the whole Senate took Jovianus and made him Emperor in place of Julian; now Jovianus was a believer, and he had been a man of God from his youth. He freed immediately the holy men, Basilius, the pillar of truth, the Cappadocian, and the brethren. Thus then, according to the word of Basilius, Julian did not return. In the peace of God. May the prayer and supplication of this great general, Saint Mercurius, come upon us, and may we all be saved thereby.

THE SECOND MIRACLE

It came to pass after seven days, during which all the multitude of the city had eaten and drunk and had kept the festival with exceedingly great joy because of the manifestation of the body of the saint, that the father of the maiden to whom the saint had given the light went to the bishop and asked him for holy baptism. When the bishop had appointed to him a certain number of days in which to fast, he baptized him and his entire household, in the name of the Father, and of the Son, and of the Holy Spirit. When the number of his family who had received baptism with him was made openly clear, it was found that fifty-three souls had been baptized that day.

After all these things, behold, Saint Mercurius appeared to the poor man as he did formerly, and he said to him, "Why are you lying here, leading a life of ease? Why do you not get up and make bricks for my shrine?" The man said to him, "My lord, I am a poor man, I have no workmen, I have neither beasts to ease my burden nor money for the expenses of the construction." The saint said to him, "I will give to you whatever you need, only you must remain a poor man. When you go into my house, if you have no doubt in your mind, you shall see my power. When you have risen up early tomorrow morning, come to the eastern part of the first of the quarters of the city, and you shall find there the young man who owns a mule. He is hoping to meet you and to talk about my body. Say to him, "Whatever you have in your hand give to me, for I need it." He shall give to you three oboli, which he is wishing to give as alms. Assuredly I will not permit you to lack anything, and they shall bring money to you in such a quantity that you will not know what to do with it. If he asks you, "How did you know that I have anything in my hand?" say to him, "It was Mercurius, who healed you, it was he who told me to speak to you."

Moreover, the young man shall speak to his father, saying, "You know at the moment when you entreated me how I made haste, listened to you, and how I gave light (i.e. sight) to your daughter. Again, I gave you your son, safe and sound. If there is anything that is lacking, make use of your friend the martyr, for the honour of a friend rests upon a friend and the martyr is accustomed to performing abundantly. For tomorrow, however, this is abundance. If he gives work to you, do it; if he will not hear you, feed yourself on the three oboli until we come to you, by the will of God, for I will come to you again and will not tarry." When the saint had said these things to him he came out from him in peace. When the morning of the next day had come, the poor man rose up, and he walked into the first quarter of the city, and came upon the young man, took from him the three oboli, and told him everything which Saint Mercurius had said to him in the dream. The young man went and told his father in fear. When his father had heard these things, he glorified God and His holy martyr Saint Mercurius. He was not unmindful in the least degree, for he made ready his camels, a large number of hired workmen and a large number of wagons. He collected a very large quantity of materials for building and delivered them over into the hands of the poor man so that the men might make bricks. He gave him tools for digging up the ground, and everything which he needed.

It came to pass on a certain day that, while the beasts were occupied in ploughing, suddenly one of the oxen attacked the other, and gored him with his horns. When the poor man saw what had happened he was grieved, and he said, "Woe to me because of this thing, for the ruler's servant has slain his beast! If only I had never delivered this dream to the young man, and if only he had not told it to his father, because he trusted me in this matter, and now this serious calamity has come upon me." While he was saying these things, behold, Saint Mercurius took the form of an ruler of the city and came out for a walk. He saw the poor man, went up to him and pretending to be surprised at what he saw said to him, "O man, why did you let your beasts be so close together that one of them could gore the other? His master will hold you liable for him." The labourer grieved exceedingly, yet he glorified the God of Saint Mercurius. When the people to whom the ox belonged heard of this, they came to see what had happened. They were exceedingly sorrowful, because the animal was a very fine one, and was very strong. Saint Mercurius was sitting some way off. No one saw him except the poor man. A very large number of people collected around the animal, and they took him into the city, into a place where he would be by himself. They put food before him to make him eat, but he would not taste the food at all. His master was grieved about him, for he was a powerful animal, and his body was godly and large. When the people had departed to their houses the poor man remained behind and was alone with the animal. He was exceedingly sorrowful, and he was meditating upon his poverty. Suddenly, behold, Saint Mercurius came in, and

he smiled a holy smile, stood up by the side of the animal of
the poor man because he was in the habit of appearing to
him face to face. The saint said to him with a smile, "You
have not delayed in becoming exhausted, O brother." The
man said to him, "Come, and see what has happened." After
these things, Saint Mercurius moved the ox with his feet, and
he said to him, "In the Name of Jesus the Christ, my Lord,
rise up, and perform your work without suffering." The ox
rose up with great vigour, just as if he had not received any
injury whatsoever, and he ate some of the grass that was
there. Straightway Saint Mercurius rebuked the ox which
had fought with the other ox, and he said to him, "Your horn
shall fall out of your head, and you shall never again have
the power to drive it into any man or animal, and you shalt
be gentle forevermore." Immediately his horn withered away
and fell out of his head, and he became gentle and docile. The
poor man cast himself down before Saint Mercurius, and said
to him, "I thank you, O my lord Mercurius, you martyr of
Christ Jesus, for the sake of whose Holy Name you became a
martyr". Immediately, Saint Mercurius hid (i.e. disappeared)
from him. The man came out, rejoicing and saying, "Saint
Mercurius has appeared to me and has healed the ox, and
has rebuked the quarrelsome animal that attacked him." The
multitude came to see what had taken place, and they all

cried out, "One is the God of Saint Mercurius. Glory be to Him forever and ever. Amen."

And it came to pass after these things that the people began to work at the making of bricks for the shrine of Saint Mercurius, and behold, the pagan ruler himself came and put himself near the workmen who were making the bricks for the shrine of Saint Mercurius. He quickly prepared for himself a place on his property for making bricks, which was near theirs, for he wished to build an entrance hall to his house. He came one day and sat down by the workmen who were making bricks for him, rose up and examined the bricks, and when he came to the bricks that were being made for the saint he felt that he would rather have a few of those than all his own put together. He said, moreover, within himself "I will carry away one hundred loads of these bricks which are made by the Christians, and I will give orders to the workmen to set them aside for me. If they say we cannot permit you to take them away, I will beat them, and then carry away the bricks by force, I will see what this person Mercurius shall do to me." He departed to his house on that day. When a few days had passed he went and looked at the bricks being made for the saint, and he sighed deeply because both the small and great in the city had turned themselves into day-laborers because they were eager to help in building the shrine for the saint. Moreover, the alien pagan coveted with great covetousness which was of the devil, the bricks of the holy man. After these things, he called to the poor man to whom Saint Mercurius used to appear, and he said to him, "Come, show me the limit of my stack of bricks and of yours, for I wish to add a building to my house." The man said to him, "Your men know the number of your bricks." The ruler said to him, "I have taken no man with me except yourself but according to my own opinion, up to this place the bricks belong to me." The poor man became terrified, and said to the pagan, "Do not punish your own soul and do not lay a finger on the bricks of this holy man, lest some calamity befall you. Nevertheless, if you are determined to take them, I know your might and your strength." The pagan struck the poor man a blow, and said to him, "It is not as you say. That one (i.e. the saint) shall strike a blow at you, and I shall carry away more than these, then I shall know your strength, and the strength of that one, what he will do to me." The poor man said to him "Do whatever pleases you. Behold, the God of Saint Mercurius is looking at you, and you will certainly not overcome Him." The ruler straightway, with arrogance, sent a message to his servant, and he sent and brought camels. He walked before them in a haughty manner, and he loaded the camels with the bricks of the saint. As he was standing before a very large male camel which belonged to him, he ordered with great arrogance his servant to load this camel with bricks, and he said, "Let me now see the power of this Mercurius." Immediately, before the words finished from his mouth, the camel in front of which he was standing opened his mouth and gripped the pagan ruler with his teeth, threw him on the ground, and rolled on him. Saint Mercurius came riding upon his horse of the spirit and drove his spear into the ruler's left leg, the leg which the camel has seized the ruler by. Whilst the ruler was being dragged into the shrine, he cried out for forgiveness to Mercurius saying, "My lord, Saint Mercurius, forgive me because of my ignorance, I will give to you all my bricks for the building of your shrine. I will give you the finest wood of every kind, and all the materials which I have collected in my house, and all the members of my house shall become Christians. I will set at liberty my servants, and they shall become free men, and I myself will become the door-keeper of your shrine until the day of my death." When the man had said these words, Saint Mercurius laid his hands upon his wounds, and he healed him, set him free, and there was no sign of any wound whatsoever in all his body. Great fear fell upon everyone who had been standing by and looking on while the camel was inflicting wounds on the ruler. The ruler confessed before them and said, "I saw Saint Mercurius driving his spear into me," but when the man examined his body he could not find in it the mark of any wound whatsoever. And the people enquired of him saying "Where is the wound in your body? Surely you cried out saying, "Behold the righteous man speared me in my legs with his spear." The ruler said to them, "From the very moment when the camel dropped me, the saint laid his hands upon all my body, I became healed." Immediately the ruler went to the bishop, who baptized him, and all the people of his house. He gave to the shrine of the saint all the materials which he had collected for the building of his own house; the wood, the stone, and all his bricks. He sent them into the shrine, together with fine gold, and many cart-loads of materials. He himself worked with his own hands among the workmen, and all his men did likewise. He said to those who were working, "Continue, and build the house of this mighty man." He died, according to the fate of all men, before the martyrium was completed. Glory be to God, and to His holy martyr Saint Mercurius.

THE THIRD MIRACLE

And it came to pass that when the building of the martyrium of Saint Mercurius had once been begun, it progressed rapidly, for the materials were abundant, and the workmen on the shrine of the saint were many. After these things, a certain man in the city came and walked about the shrine, and when he saw the timber and bricks for the shrine of the martyrium he marvelled, and he coveted some of the wood which was lying about. He said, "I have need of this fine plank of wood." He went to where the wood was and lifted it up on his back, and he walked away with it until he came to within a short distance of the city. He then lost his way and did not know where he was walking, because the saint had made his mind to wander. He came and stood at the door of the poor man, the steward of Saint Mercurius, to whom the saint used to appear. Now the man who had stolen the wood did not know where he was going. Behold the saint spoke to the steward and said to him, "What are you doing sitting here idle? Behold, the wood is being stolen from my shrine! Rise up, and go to the door of your house, and there you will find the man with the wood on his back, he is staggering about here and there, and he does not know where he is going. Now it is I who have made him lose his way, and I

have prevented him from knowing where he was going until
he came to this place. You will see him there carrying the
wood which he has stolen." When the thief saw the house
in front of him and that one had opened the door to him, he
recognized that the opener of the door was the steward of
the martyrium, for his understanding had returned to him.
Immediately he cried out, saying, "One is the God of Saint
Mercurius! Have mercy upon me, and do not be angry with
me, do not bring evil upon me. I have sinned against you and
I have stolen your wood." Behold, the saint spoke again to
the steward, saying, "Speak to the man in this way: Why did
you dare to come and commit this outrageous robbery at my
shrine? Moreover, the wood which you stole was given to my
shrine by men for the redemption and salvation of their souls.
But through the compassion of God, behold, I will set you
free. Take the wood and carry it away and lay it in the place
wherein you found it, and then go to your own house. When
the morning has come, let him proclaim what I have done to
him, in order that others may fear, and may not again steal
the building materials from my shrine, lest I bring evil upon
them." When the saint had said these things, he disappeared
from the steward.

The poor man rose up and came forth, and he found the

man with the wood on his back, standing by the door of his house; now the thief did not know where he had come to. He was saying, "O Saint Mercurius, have compassion upon me, and have mercy upon me, for I have sinned, O my lord." The poor man spoke to him, saying, "O my beloved brother, where have come from carrying this wood on your back? I say to you this wood belongs to Saint Mercurius; moreover, tell me all that has happened to you." The man told him how he had carried off the wood, and how Saint Mercurius had made his mind to wander so much that he at length arrived at the door of the house of the poor man without knowing what he was doing. The man to whom Saint Mercurius was accustomed to appearing announced to the man who had stolen the wood everything which Saint Mercurius had declared to him. When the thief had heard these words he marveled and said, "I will not do it for one day only, but if the God of Saint Mercurius will graciously grant me health, I will never cease to labor at his shrine until it is finished. I will proclaim his mighty power in every place I go." His senses returned to him, and he departed to his house, glorified God and His holy martyr, and he lay down and slept until the morning.

When daylight appeared, the thief proclaimed in the

entire city what had happened. He went to the place where the wood had been brought, lifted it up on his shoulders. Now everyone was looking at him and he carried it to the shrine of the saint and laid it down in the place from which he had taken it. Great fear fell upon everyone who saw him, and no other man again laid a hand upon any other material for the shrine until it was completed. The man who had stolen the wood did not cease to toil in mixing mud and making bricks for the shrine of the saint until the building was completed.

THE FOURTH MIRACLE

Listen also, O my beloved, to the following great miracle, which is to the glory of the God of Saint Mercurius. It came to pass that when the building of the shrine had been successfully finished, and it had been beautified with adornments of every kind, they made and placed in it a screen (or, grating) made of shouebe wood. Now there were three large shouebe trees which were the property of the woman to whom Saint Mercurius had given the light, and these had belonged to her blessed husband, who before his death had intended them to be made into a large kinbêl. Besides these, when God visited him before his death, he left very large possessions to her. Straightaway the apse was made of good and sound shouebe wood. When a very large number of men had been gathered together to lift it up into its place, a few of the workmen said among themselves in a jesting manner, "I really do wish that the heart of Saint Mercurius would be gracious to us who are building his martyrium and that he would make the shouebe-wood apse to put forth branches, laden with fruit just as if it were growing, so that we might eat of it." Suddenly, whilst they were still speaking, the wood sent forth branches laden with very fine ripe fruit. When the multitude saw what had taken place they cried out with a loud voice and glorified God and His holy martyr who does great and marvellous things. A certain zealous man brought away some of the fruit and kept it for themselves in their houses as a reminder. O how very many were the cures which were performed by means of that fruit! The multitudes ate and drank, and gave thanks to God and to His holy martyr, Saint Mercurius. Every person who was in the city and in its neighborhood, both small and great, heard of this, and they came with one accord to see a great miracle. Both men and women came and saw what had happened by the righteous man.

There was in the city a certain Jew who was called Gaipios who behaved in an uncivilized and savage manner to every man, especially to the Christians. He too heard of the wonderful thing which had taken place in the shrine of the saint, and he said, "I will go and see if these things which these Christians are saying are true or not, perhaps they are telling lies." He commanded one of his slaves to saddle a mule and he said to his servant, "Come, and let us see the stupid fraud which the Christians are celebrating." Immediately they set out together and went on until they came to the shrine of Saint Mercurius. One of the Christian young men who cleaned and tended the shrine said to him, "Where are you going, O godless man, with this beast? Will you go into the church of God riding upon a mule?" The Jew paid not the smallest regard to him, or to his words, but he went in and stood still, and looked up into the apse, which was laden with fruit and leaves that seemed to be growing upon a tree in the ground. The Jew said, "Who is it that has been adding leaves which are out of season to the crowns? They tell lies about the saint in saying that it is he who has done this." The incorruptible young man, who had at first spoken to the Jew about bringing the beast upon which he was riding into the shrine, answered and said to him, "He who will destroy you immediately, is he who makes manifest all the miracles." Straightaway the Jew was filled with wrath, and in a mighty passion, he rode his beast at the young man in order to trample him under foot. The feet of the mule sank down into the ground as if it had been mud, and the Jew fell upon his face, cut himself on the stones and bricks which were lying scattered about on the floor of the building. Behold, straightaway Saint Mercurius came to the door, accompanied by an angel. He was holding his spear in his hand. He said to the Jew, "What are you doing in this place? This place is not one in which to stable beasts, though you have brought your mule into it. The leaves (or foliage) are out of season, and so likewise is the fruit. You have come into this place for the purpose of driving away those who are working at my shrine. You will neither work yourself for me nor will you let others work." The saint thrust his spear into the middle of the body of the Jew, and his bowels came out, but no man saw the saint except the Jew, whom the saint was piercing. All they saw was a man lying stretched out upon the ground in a state of unconsciousness, knowing nothing whatsoever about what had happened to him.

And it came to pass that after a time the Jew cried out with a loud voice, saying, "O Saint Mercurius, help me in this hour of necessity, and I will never again be ignorant concerning any of the saint's deeds. If you will show mercy to me, and bring me out of this sickness, I will become a Christian. I will make and dedicate a statue to you on which you shall be represented in all your glory. I will make you appear as you are now, with your spear thrust into me; I will also make a figure of myself lying prostrate under your feet, in great shame and helplessness. I will gild your figure with the finest gold and will inlay it with precious stones which shall sparkle like fire, that is to say, with chrysolites, and the figure of your spear I will inlay with precious stones of great price, that is to say, with diamonds. Help me, O my lord Mercurius." Having said these words, he fell back prostrate and lay there half dead.

After these things the angel of the Lord spoke to Saint Mercurius, saying, "Withdraw your spear from him, if he will truly believe in our King the Christ. Far better is the sinner who repents that he has sinned than a righteous man, and there is joy among the angels over a sinner who shall repent of his sins even according to what the Saviour told His disciples when He was with them, saying, "Let Your mercy come to him, for he is without knowledge." The saint released the Jew. When his senses returned to him, he related to the multitude that was gathered together everything that had happened to him, and they glorified God who worked these miracles by the hand of His holy martyr.

After these things, the man rose up and departed to his

house, and he related to his wife and servants everything that had happened to him. Now he had no son, for his wife was barren. On the next day, he said to his wife, "Whatever God will let it come to me." He took his wife and his servants, and he went to the bishop, who baptized them in the Name of the Father, and of the Son, and of the Holy Spirit. The bishop called the name of the Jew Zacharias and that of his wife Elizabeth. When he had gone into his house he knew his wife, and she conceived. When nine months were fulfilled, she brought forth male twins. She called the first-born Mercurius, after the name of the saint, because she said, "I have obtained salvation through him;" and the second she called John, after the name of the Baptist. After all these things the Jew summoned an artist and gave to him ten pounds of fine gold, and a number of very fine precious stones and the artist made a portrait figure of Saint Mercurius, holding in his hand his spear, which was inlaid with diamonds. He made also a figure of himself in gold, inlaid with precious stones, lying at the feet of Saint Mercurius, who was thrusting his spear into his body. The Jew took this statue into the church, and after it had been consecrated at the shrine he deposited it in the sanctuary, where it remains to this day. It is to this moment a testimony of the miracles of the holy martyr, Saint Mercurius.

THE FIFTH MIRACLE

As years went on the fame of the saint grew. Multitudes thronged to his shrine to worship his relics and to make offerings to him; and those who were sick were healed, and devils were cast out, and every believing sufferer obtained relief. Among the noblemen of the district was one called Hermapollo, who had only one child, a little daughter, and she was the object of his deepest affection. Hearing of the miracles of the saint, he made a journey to his shrine, and prayed there for his daughter's welfare. He gave thirty oboli to the shrine and thirty oboli to the steward thereof. The clergy of the shrine were hospitable men, and they entertained the nobleman at dinner and pleased him, wherefore he promised to present to the shrine of the saint a bier, or couch of state, upon which the relics of the saint could be carried in procession with suitable honour through the streets of his town. Hermapollo slept in the shrine that night, and St. Mercurius appeared to him there in the form of a general and promised to give him a son-in-law if he would give without fail the couch of state which he had promised to his shrine. When morning came Hermapollo paid a final visit to the relics of the saint and returned to his home.

Shortly after his return a nobleman of the district sent messengers to Hermapollo asking him to give his daughter to his son to wife. Hermapollo's wife received the messengers and heard the proposals which they made in respect of the dowry , and then laid the matter before her husband. The offer was unsatisfactory in Hermapollo's opinion and was rejected, and the messengers returned to their master sadly. That evening the parents of the young man for whom the maiden was asked, told him that their attempt to obtain her for him had failed, and tried to pursuade him to transfer his affections to another maiden, but none of the maidens whose names were mentioned by them pleased him. He was desperately in love with Hermapollo's daughter and found means to communicate with her by writing. He lay awake at night inventing schemes for obtaining possession of the maiden. Soon after the mother of the young man had made the proposal of marriage for her son she died, and her husband, being overcome with grief, took no further steps in the search for a wife for his son.

Meanwhile the young man could not forget the maiden whom he loved, and his distress of mind was so great that he fell into bad health, a sickness nearing death. At length, he considered the use of magic for his purpose, and he applied to one magician after another, asking them to use their powers in such a way that the parents of the maiden might accept his suit. Finally, he found a great magician who promised to bring the maiden to him, so that he might see her face to face and talk with her. The magician cast a spell on the young maiden, causing an evil spirit to take possession of her. Hermapollo wanting his daughter to be healed, took her to the shrine of Mercurius to have the spirit expelled. About this time the couch of state which Hermapollo had promised to give to the shrine was completed, and taking it, and his wife and sick daughter, he set out from his house for the shrine. When he arrived with his family and the priests saw the splendour of his gift they marvelled. The framework of the couch rested on pillars which were set upon pedestals, and it was decorated with inlaid leaves of ivory, and with a figure of the martyr made of precious stones, six crosses, three of gold and three of silver. When Mercurius saw the sad plight of the daughter of Hermapollo, he went to the town where lived the young man who wished to marry her and appeared to him by night in the form of a general with his sword drawn in his hand. When the young man woke up and saw the wrathful face of the saint he was terrified. When he had been smitten thrice with the flat side of the sword he fell on his knees and begged for mercy. The saint rebuked him severely for causing a spell to be cast on Hermapollo's daughter but agreed to spare his life on condition that he went to the magician in the morning and made him remove the spell which he had cast upon the maiden. He also promised the young man happiness when he should come to his shrine.

On the following morning, the young man set out for the shrine of Mercurius but stopped at the village where the magician lived in order to tell him all that had happened. When the magician heard that Hermapollo and his daughter were in the shrine of Mercurius he was afraid, and would not go with the young man, who proceeded to enter alone. As soon as he arrived in the shrine he gave the steward ten oboli. When he looked around he saw the maiden whom he loved lying close to the body of the saint, and her father and mother weeping, requesting his help and relief for their daughter, which were granted to her. When Hermapollo looked around, and saw the young man there, he recognized him, and going to him asked him concerning his parents' health. Knowing nothing about the young man's connection with the magician and the spell which had been cast on his daughter. Hermapollo took the young man to his lodgings, and made him known to his wife and daughter; and the young man ate with the family, and saw his beloved and rejoiced, although the delicate appearance of the maiden and the thought of what she had suffered grieved him sorely. That night Mercurius appeared to Hermapollo and told him to give his daughter to the young man, who would become of age, and would succeed his father in three months' time. He made him aware that it was he who had caused the maiden to fall ill through his great longing for her. Early the next morning Hermapollo and his family and the young man went into the sanctuary to worship. Hermapollo was hoping that the saint would clear up the matter of his daughter's marriage. When the young man went to the couch of state to admire it, he found the magician tied to it, like a dog, and the wretched man told him that Mercurius first gagged him and then dragged him to the shrine and tied him up there. Whilst they were talking, a devil leaped upon the magician, having orders to punish him for the blasphemies which he had uttered, and Mercurius, having driven out of him another devil, restored his sight to him and dismissed him to the desert, where he lived there after. When the Eucharist was taken, it was found that all pain had left Hermapollo's daughter. A woman who was possessed of a spirit cried out to Hermapollo, telling him to give his daughter in marriage to the young man, for her one hope of permanent cure lay in her marriage with him. After the festival Hermapollo, his family and the young man travelled back to their native city together. Shortly afterwards the marriage of the young man with the maiden was arranged, and the ceremony was performed with great pomp and splendour and rejoicing. Within three months from the wedding the father of the bridegroom died and left all his property to his son. As a mark of gratitude to Mercurius for his assistance, the daughter of Hermapollo and her husband paid annual visits to his shrine.